BRIGHT IDEA BOOKS

FRANKENSTEIN'S
Monster

by Marie Pearson

raintree
a Capstone company — publishers for children

Raintree is an imprint of Capstone Global Library Limited, a company incorporated in England and Wales having its registered office at 264 Banbury Road, Oxford, OX2 ?DY - Registered company number: 6695582

www.raintree.co.uk
myorders@raintree.co.uk

Editor: Claire Vanden Branden
Designer: Becky Daum
Production Specialist: Laura Manthe
Originated by Capstone Global Library Limited
Printed and bound in India

ISBN 978 1 4747 8765 9 (hardback)
ISBN 978 1 4747 8775 8 (paperback)

British Library Cataloguing in Publication Data
A full catalogue record for this book is available from the British Library

Acknowledgements
We would like to thank the following for permission to reproduce photographs: Alamy: Universal Pictures/Ronald Grant Archive, 14–15, World History Archive, 24; iStockphoto: PatriciaPix, cover (foreground), PietroPazzi, 18–19, RetroAtelier, 16–17; Newscom: Columbia Pictures/Sony Pictures Animation/Album, 23; North Wind Picture Archives: 5; Shutterstock Images: Anton_Ivanov, 13, 29, carrie-nelson, 26–27, Iurii Buriak, 6–7, Kiwi Rik, 30–31, Marafona, cover (background), Mkilroy, 9, Tero Vesalainen, 10–11, Terry Kelly, 21, 28
Design Elements: Shutterstock Images, Red Line Editorial

CONTENTS

CHAPTER 1

BIRTH OF A
Monster

The year was 1816. Mary Wollstonecraft Godwin was staying in Switzerland with some friends. She was 18 years old. One of these friends was Percy Shelley. They would later marry and Mary would become Mary Shelley.

Mary Shelley is known as the Queen of Horror for the scary stories she wrote.

The friends talked about science. Scientists had been studying if dead things could be brought back to life. Then the friends decided to each write a scary story. Shelley wrote *Frankenstein*. It was published two years later.

200 YEARS

The year 2018 was the 200th **anniversary** of *Frankenstein*. People around the world read the book at Halloween.

A castle in Germany is thought to be Shelley's inspiration for *Frankenstein*.

Mary's book is about Victor Frankenstein. He is **obsessed** with finding the key to **eternal** life. One day he finds the answer. He starts creating a creature. He wants to bring it to life. The creature looks similar to a human. It has two legs and two arms. It has hair on its head. But it is much bigger than a human. Frankenstein finishes making the creature. He thinks the creature is beautiful.

It took nearly two years for Victor Frankenstein to make the creature.

9

Then Frankenstein brings the creature to life. But he is terrified. He has achieved his goal. But the creature is not beautiful. He is **hideous**. Frankenstein had been too obsessed to see this. Now he sees that the creature is ugly and scary. Frankenstein runs and hides.

It doesn't say in the book, but many people think the creature was brought to life using electricity.

CHAPTER 2

ON THE
Run

The creature Frankenstein made is alone. His creator has abandoned him. Life is hard for him. Everyone who sees him is afraid.

The creature felt
very alone when
Frankenstein left him.

The creature hides. A family lives in a home near the creature's hiding place. The creature listens to them. He learns human language. One of the men is blind. The creature waits until everyone else is gone. Then he tries to talk to the man. Maybe the man won't be scared.

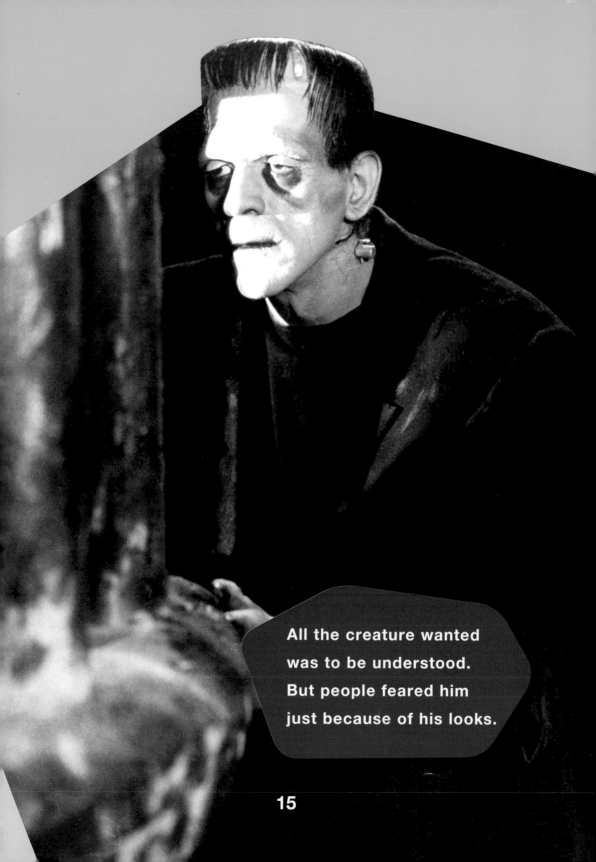

All the creature wanted
was to be understood.
But people feared him
just because of his looks.

The creature's partner is often shown as a woman who has black hair with white streaks.

16

The creature approaches the man. But the man's son comes back. He thinks the creature is going to hurt his dad. The son beats the creature. The family escapes from the house.

The creature is angry and burns the house down. He wants someone to love him. He finds Frankenstein. He asks his creator to make a female so he won't be alone. Frankenstein agrees.

Frankenstein starts to make a
female, but then he stops. He doesn't
want the creatures to have children.
They could spread through the world.
He decides to destroy the female.

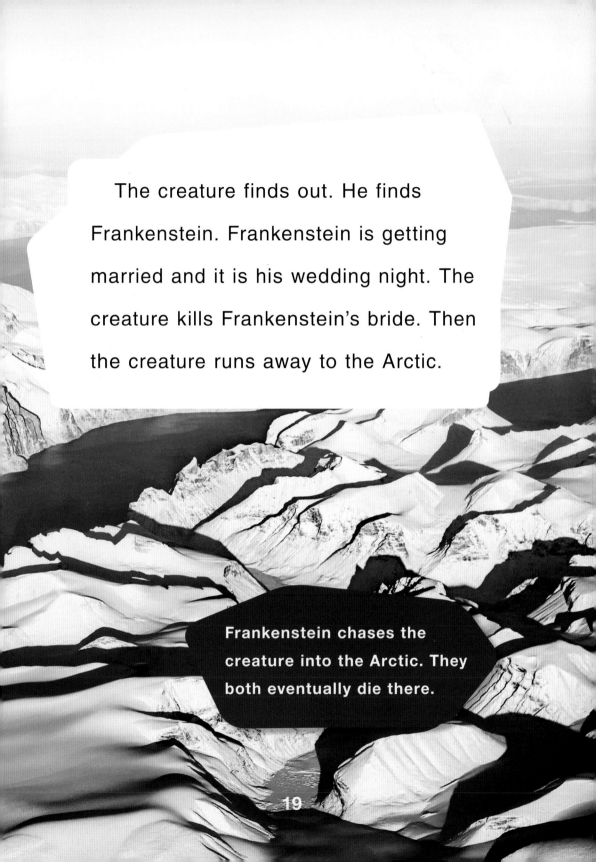

The creature finds out. He finds Frankenstein. Frankenstein is getting married and it is his wedding night. The creature kills Frankenstein's bride. Then the creature runs away to the Arctic.

Frankenstein chases the creature into the Arctic. They both eventually die there.

19

CHAPTER 3

ABOUT THE
Creature

People around the world know the name Frankenstein. Many think that is the creature's name. But it is actually the name of the man who created him. The creature has no name. His creator never gave him one.

The creature has black hair and white teeth. His skin is thin. It is a sickly yellow colour. The creature can run faster than a human and is much stronger too.

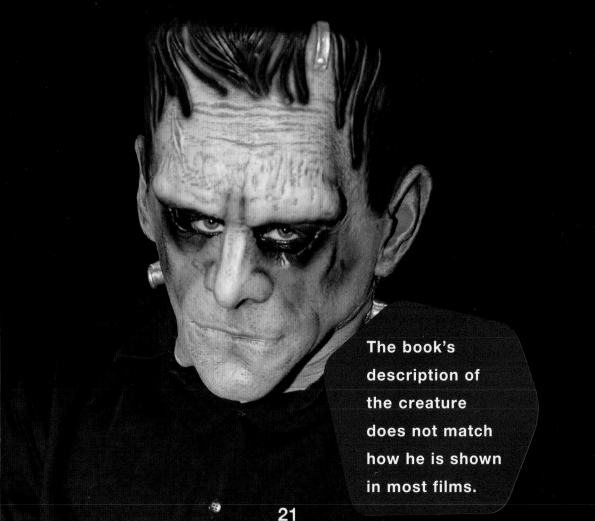

The book's description of the creature does not match how he is shown in most films.

CHAPTER 4

THE MONSTER'S
Influence

Many people today have one image of Frankenstein's monster in their minds. They think of the cartoon image of the creature's face. His skin is green. He is covered in stitches. These **represent** how his body was pieced together. Sometimes there are screws in his neck.

Frankenstein's monster is still used in popular movies today, such as *Hotel Transylvania 3.*

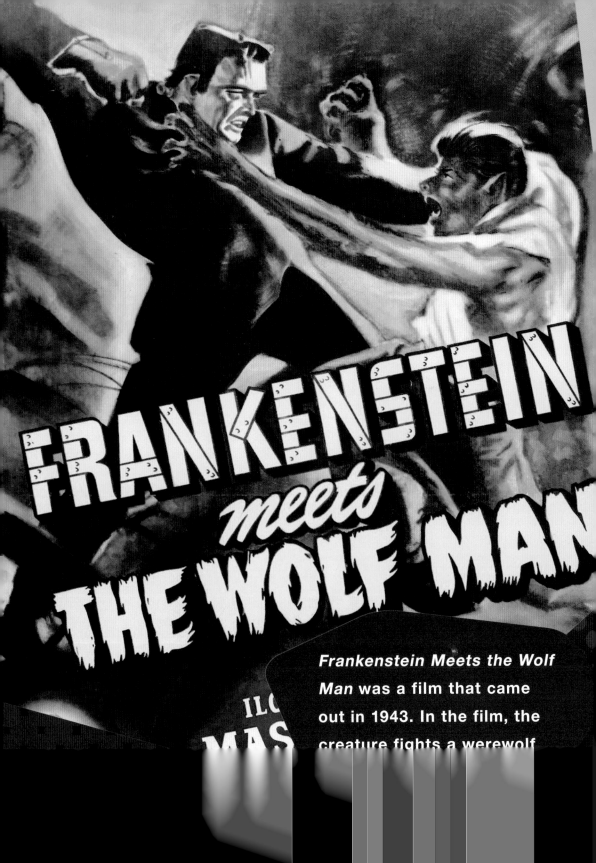

FRANKENSTEIN *meets* THE WOLF MAN

ILC
MAS

Frankenstein Meets the Wolf *Man* was a film that came out in 1943. In the film, the creature fights a werewolf

Today, Frankenstein's monster is in many stories and films. Sometimes he is evil. Sometimes he fights other monsters.

But he has also been a superhero. Marvel made a comic book about the creature. He faces other superheroes in the series.

HORROR FICTION

Mary Shelley was the first creator of **horror fiction.** Many people wrote scary stories after Shelley.

The *Frankenstein* story has a lesson. It makes people question a scientist's responsibility. Scientists can do amazing things, but they can also make dangerous things. They need to be responsible for their inventions. If they don't, people could get hurt.

Mary Shelley told the original story of Frankenstein's creature. Today *Frankenstein* continues to interest people around the world.

People today still enjoy dressing up as Frankenstein's monster at Halloween.

GLOSSARY

anniversary
the date of an important event that can be observed every year

eternal
going on forever

hideous
extremely ugly

horror fiction
a type of fiction story that is intended to scare readers

obsess
to fill your mind with something all of the time

represent
to indicate or stand for something else or a greater meaning

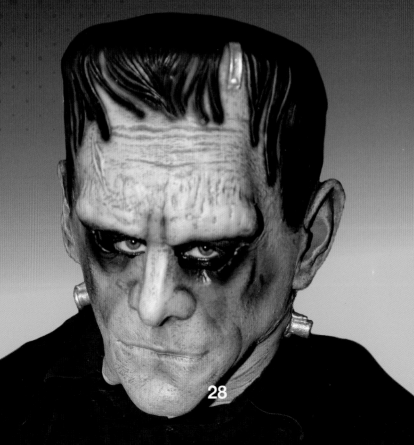

TRIVIA

1. Mary's husband, Percy Shelley, was a poet. He made some contributions to Mary's novel *Frankenstein*.

2. Mary had a nightmare about a man's body. A machine started up, and the body began moving uneasily. She used this nightmare to inspire the creation of the creature in her novel.

3. *Frankenstein* wasn't popular with critics at the time it was published. Five years after the book was published, a play was made based on the book. It wasn't until this time that the story really became popular.

ACTIVITY

A HERO OR A VILLAIN?

Look closely at the actions of Frankenstein in this book. He built a creature without thinking about how the monster would behave in the world. Many people think Frankenstein's monster was the hero. They say he didn't do anything wrong. The scientist was actually the monster. But others think the creature was evil because he killed people. What do you think? Write a one-page essay on whether you think the monster is the hero or the villain. Use at least two sources to back up your thoughts. Then present your paper to your family or friends.

31

FIND OUT MORE

Want to learn more about *Frankenstein*? Check out the following resources:

British Library: Mary Shelley
www.bl.uk/people/mary-shelley

Frankenstein (Graphic Revolve), Mary Shelley, retold by Michael Burgan
(Raintree, 2009)

Kids Connect: Frankenstein facts and worksheets
kidskonnect.com/social-studies/frankenstein/

Want to find out more about science related to the book? Look at these sources:

Nature: science fiction: the science that fed *Frankenstein*
www.nature.com/articles/535490a

Video: PBS: the real "Doctor Frankenstein"
www.pbs.org/video/its-okay-be-smart-frankenstein

INDEX